Broken and Poured Out

✠ ✠ ✠

A Spirituality for Eucharistic Ministers

Richard R. Gaillardetz, Ph.D.

Liguori
ONE LIGUORI DRIVE
LIGUORI MO 63057-9999

Imprimi Potest:
Richard Thibodeau, C.Ss.R.
Provincial, Denver Province
The Redemptorists

ISBN 0-7648-0772-2
© 2002, Liguori Publications
Printed in the United States of America
02 03 04 05 06 5 4 3 2 1

To order, call 1-800-325-9521
www.liguori.org
www.catholicbooksonline.com

Contents

✠ ✠ ✠

Introduction / 5

Eucharistic Ministers Are First
  Liturgical Ministers / 7

Servants of the Mystery:
  Recovering Traditional
  Eucharistic Doctrine / 17

    Eucharistic Real Presence / 17
    The Eucharist as Sacrifice / 25

"Receive What You Are" / 33

The Eucharist and the Reign of God / 37

Extending Table Fellowship:
  Communion with the Sick / 41

Conclusion / 45

About the Author

Dr. Richard R. Gaillardetz holds the Margaret and Thomas Murray and James J. Bacik Endowed Chair in Catholic Studies at the University of Toledo in Toledo, Ohio. He has published numerous articles and authored or edited five books, including *A Daring Promise: A Spirituality of Christian Marriage* (Crossroad, 2002). He is currently a Catholic delegate on the U.S. Catholic-Methodist Dialogue and a past (2000) recipient of the Washington Theological Union's Sophia Award, offered in recognition of "theological excellence in service to ministry." Dr. Gaillardetz is a popular speaker at theological and pastoral conferences and is married and the father of four young boys.

Introduction

✠ ✠ ✠

I still recall the first few months after the Vatican gave lay people permission to distribute the Eucharist during Mass. There stood our pastor on one side and the extraordinary minister of the Eucharist alongside of him. The lay minister had about ten people in his line while large numbers crossed over to receive Communion from the priest. Most of us chuckle at such reminiscences. We are certainly a long way from that early suspicion; extraordinary ministers of the Eucharist (I will refer to these simply as lay eucharistic ministers) are now widely accepted in the Church. Most of us feel quite honored when we are invited by our community or its pastor to serve in this important ministry. We sense, rightly, that we are participating in something important and sacred. I wish to offer some reflections on why this ministry

is important and how we can cultivate a spirituality appropriate to this ministry.

Eucharistic Ministers Are
First Liturgical Ministers

✠ ✠ ✠

When lay eucharistic ministers are asked about the doctrinal significance of their ministry, most speak immediately of the Catholic belief in the real presence of Christ in the Eucharist. Obviously, this doctrine is vital to our understanding of the spirituality of the lay eucharistic minister. However, lay eucharistic ministers do more than simply distribute Communion; it is important to relate their ministry to the whole liturgical action of the community in prayer.

The *Catechism of the Catholic Church* (henceforward, CCC) begins its discussion of the Eucharist not with the doctrine of the real presence but with a consideration of the eucharistic liturgy as a whole. In that important catechetical resource, the traditional understanding of eucharistic real presence and sacrifice is placed in the larger context of the Eucharist as a liturgical action of the whole assembly under the presidency of the priest.[1] The root meaning of the word *liturgy* is *the public work of the people.* Catholic Christians believe that the Christian liturgy is in fact "the participation of the People of God in 'the work of God'" (*CCC* 1069).

This larger liturgical context is important because we live in a consumerist culture that turns all of the goods we value into prepackaged commodities. In this cultural milieu we find it all too easy to treat the Eucharist as itself a kind of commodity, a sacred object to be distributed and then consumed. This approach inclines us to view the ministry of the eucharistic minister strictly in terms of distributing these sacred objects to the faithful. However, if the starting point for our reflection is the liturgical action of the community, our focus shifts to consider how eucharistic ministers serve the larger movement of the entire liturgy.

What is it we are really doing when we participate in the liturgy? For some the liturgy is a mere extension of their own private prayer and devotions. Their view of the liturgy is guilty of a kind of verticalism that focuses so much on their individual relationship to God that the presence of the rest of the community becomes irrelevant. Two complementary images come to mind.

Imagine hundreds of different phone booths under the same church roof, with each occupied by an individual believer seeking to establish a private line of communication to God that goes through the altar as a common switchboard. What matters is what transpires within one's own phone booth; the activity in the other phone booths in this church can only be a nuisance and a distraction. Here the priest, and indeed all the liturgical ministers, are little more than switchboard operators trying to bring about each believer's private phone connection. Another image would be that of the church as a religious supermarket in which individuals go in search of a particular product they perceive they need—in this instance, the eucharistic elements. This image, as with the previous one, suggests that again the eucharistic celebration is primarily a private affair, now between the "spiritual consumer" and God.

Within this imaginative framework, the priest
and other liturgical ministers are like supermarket cashiers dispensing a desired commodity. How often have we gone up to Communion and received the consecrated host or
cup from the priest, deacon, or lay eucharistic minister in a way all too reminiscent of
the experience of being handed our grocer-
ies by a cashier or bagger with no personal
exchange and no eye contact.

At the other end of the spectrum is a liturgical horizontalism. This approach has been
fashioned, for the most part, as a reaction to
the verticalist sensibility. Here the liturgy is
conducted with a studied informality. The
liturgical ministers (if there are any) wear few
or no vestments and sit indistinguishably
among the whole assembly. The presidential
prayers are either improvised or recited aloud
by the whole community. Bread and cup are
passed around in a way that makes the very
presence of a eucharistic minister superflu-
ous. Congregational participation is placed
at a premium as are gestures that accentuate
horizontal solidarity, for example, holding
hands throughout much of the liturgy, making a point of extending the sign of peace to

every participant in the assembly. The respective roles of the priest-presider and other liturgical ministers are diminished when they do not disappear entirely. This kind of liturgical experience calls to mind what one might experience in a support group with no formal leader and only minimal guidelines for communal interaction.

My accounts of both liturgical verticalism and horizontalism are admittedly caricatures offered to lay out the extremes as clearly as possible. They are recounted to highlight the difference between narrow perspectives and the wealth of complementary insights into the eucharistic liturgy offered by our great tradition. Let us consider a few of these insights.

First the liturgy is a communal celebration, not merely of each individual's personal hopes and desires but of a common conviction that God has been, is now, and ever will be committed to our salvation. We participate in the liturgy as recipients of a marvelous gift, God's redemptive love, and we celebrate that in word, ritual, and symbol as we recount the history of God's saving work on behalf of humankind and all of creation. The next time you are at Mass, listen to the prayers of the liturgy (and not just during the Scripture readings of the Liturgy of the Word) and note how often they make reference to what God has done in history on our behalf. Much of the liturgy consists in retelling a shared story about how God is God-for-us.

There is a tendency among liturgical ministers to divide up their ministries according to the classical twofold division of the Liturgy of the Word and the Liturgy of the Eucharist. The result too often is a "tag team" mentality in which lectors do their part during the liturgy of the word and then "tag" the lay eucharistic ministers who then do their part in the second half of the Mass. This is a mistaken perspective, however. The "telling of the story" of the history of God's saving words and deeds does not end with the conclusion of the Liturgy of the Word but continues in the Liturgy of the Eucharist in a new key. There too God's story continues to be told in the eucharistic prayers and in the ritual action first recounted in Scripture in which bread is taken, blessed, broken, and offered. To be a lay eucharistic minister, it is vital to see one's ministry as a participation in this telling of the story of the God who pitched his tent among us in Jesus of Nazareth. The lay eucharistic minister shares in telling the story of Jesus who suffered, died, and was raised by the Father and who continues to be encountered in the breaking of the bread. To say "the body of Christ" and hand a communicant the consecrated bread, to say "the blood of Christ" and offer the cup of salvation is to continue telling the story of God's saving action, God's self-gift among and on behalf of God's people.

Because we are recipients of God's marvelous gift of salvation, we also celebrate the liturgy as an act of corporate gratitude, praise, and thanksgiving. It is easy to forget that the root meaning of the word *eucharist* is thanksgiving. "The Eucharist is a sacrifice of thanksgiving to the Father, a blessing by which the Church expresses her gratitude to God for all his benefits, for all that he has accomplished through creation, redemption, and sanctification" (*CCC* 1360). We believe that in the liturgy all Christians are spiritually united with Christ in his praise to the God of all creation. There is a spirituality of praise that can be cultivated by us all as we allow our hearts to overflow in praise to God.

All liturgical ministry is a participation in the offering of praise to God. Yet how often have we encountered eucharistic ministers whose demeanor seems so far removed from the delight of a grateful heart? Obviously their ministry demands a certain reverence, but this need not be opposed to a joyful heart. Living in the Spirit and knowing ourselves to be beloved of God, the spirit of praise and thanksgiving ought to well up within us. This movement to offer praise to God is not merely the result of our own efforts. As Saint Paul reminds us, "that very Spirit intercedes [for us] with sighs too deep for words" (Romans 8:26). This explains the peculiar logic of praise, "for praise perfects perfection."[2] Praise operates according to the logic of overflow, of giving without measure. Consider for a moment what happens when I praise another person or express my love for him or her. I might think that this expression or act of praise serves as mere gloss adding something additional to the relationship. But in fact this is not the case. The actual expression of love doesn't just add something to a preexisting relationship, it actually constitutes a new relationship. A relationship is born anew

with the offering of praise. So it is with praise
of God. The act of giving praise itself places
us in a new relationship with God. This movement to give praise and thanksgiving is itself
initiated by the Spirit who unites us with
Jesus, the one who first taught us to pray to
God. Recall the wonderful prayer in the liturgy: "Father, you have no need of our praise,
but our desire to praise you is itself your gift
to us."

As eucharistic ministers we must all learn
to see our ministry grounded not just in our
own particular tasks in the liturgy but in the
dynamism of the whole liturgy.

QUESTIONS FOR REFLECTION

*Has your own attitude toward the
liturgy been guilty of either a liturgical horizontalism or verticalism?*

*What if any of the approaches to
the liturgy mentioned above have
been neglected in the way the liturgy has been celebrated in your
experience?*

Servants of the Mystery: Recovering Traditional Eucharistic Doctrine

✠ ✠ ✠

O ur understanding of the Mass has traditionally been informed by two fundamental convictions, the first regarding the real presence of Christ in the Eucharist, and the second regarding the nature of the Eucharist as sacrifice. Let us consider these in more detail.

Eucharistic Real Presence

In its presentation of the doctrine of the Real Presence the catechism recalls the teaching of the Council of Trent that in the Eucharist "the body and blood, together with the soul and divinity, of our Lord Jesus Christ and, therefore, the whole Christ is truly, really and substantially contained" (*CCC* 1374). The Council of Trent went on to note that *transubstantiation* is a most appropriate (*aptissime*) way of explaining how this Real Presence comes to be. This means, however, that we must distinguish between orthodox belief in the Real Presence of Christ in the Eucharist and the theory of *transubstantiation,* which the Council recommends as a most apt or fitting theological explanation of that reality. I offer this because one sometimes finds an attitude in which any sentence one might utter regarding the Eucharist that does not include the word *transubstantiation* is considered doctrinally suspect. *Transubstantiation* refers to a philosophically and theologically sophisticated theory intended to explain a change in the eucharistic elements that is not physical in nature but metaphysical, or more accurately, sacramental. The theory holds that while the *substance* of the bread and wine (its deepest and most profound reality) changes to that of the body and blood of Christ, the *accidents,* the sensible appearances of the bread and wine remain. The Council affirms the suitability of using this kind of terminology for describing the eucharistic presence. It does not say that this is the only terminology or theological system one can use to speak of the Eucharist. Surely theologians can and must always search for new and perhaps even better ways to describe the reality of Christ's eucharistic presence. This is important to remember because the notion of transubstantiation is sometimes misunderstood.

One still comes across pious eucharistic literature that uses the language of transubstantiation in a manner that suggests, mistakenly, that Christ is *physically* present in the eucharistic elements. Yet both Saint Augustine and Saint Thomas Aquinas insisted that the eucharistic body of Christ was not Christ's *physical* body. Rather Christ is present in a real but spiritual manner. Explaining an important passage of Augustine, Aquinas wrote:

> *When Augustine says, "You will not be eating this body which you see," he does not intend to exclude the reality of Christ's body, what he does rule out is that they would eat it under the same form in which they were looking at*

it.... [Augustine did not mean that] the body of Christ is in this sacrament only as a "mystical symbol." Rather, he meant that Christ's body is there spiritually, that is, invisibly and by the power of the Spirit.[3]

Both Augustine and Thomas knew well that "real" was not synonymous with "physical."

To explore the significance of this distinction we might recall the story of the disciples who encountered the risen Lord on the road to Emmaus. This is a story about disciples who had to be taught the difference between physical presence and sacramental presence. Recall that after Jesus' death the disciples encounter him on the road to Emmaus but do not recognize him.[4] This failure to recognize him is quite significant. The Jesus they knew and longed for was the one with whom they walked on the shores of Galilee, the one who was tortured, crucified, and buried in a tomb. Since they were looking for *that* Jesus, the one they knew in the flesh, they could not recognize the now risen Lord who walked with them. Only after the risen Lord explained the Scriptures to them and broke bread with them did they encounter him "in the breaking of the bread." They had finally come to realize that Jesus must now be encountered in a new way, sacramentally rather than physically.

The story of Emmaus is a story about how the whole Christian community is called to encounter Jesus in a new way. This is the deep truth of Christ's ascension into heaven; he is no longer with us in the same manner. Yet many then and still today resist this and while using the language of sacrament continue to seek the *physical* Jesus who was crucified and laid in the tomb. They fail to grasp that sacramental presence is not the same as physical presence. Christ is present but now in a sacramental action in which a sense of Jesus' presence is inseparable from a sense of absence—he no longer can be encountered in the sensible, tangible way he was prior to his death and resurrection.

As humans we long for an *immediate* encounter with Jesus. This explains in part why so many are drawn to religious phenomena like the shroud of Turin and other religious "miracles." We long for a tangible proof of God's existence and presence. What God gives us however are not tangible proofs but sacramental signs that indeed make Christ present to us but in a manner visible only with the eyes of faith. Louis-Marie Chauvet claims rather pointedly that "you cannot arrive at the recognition of the risen Jesus unless you renounce seeing/touching/finding him by undeniable proofs."[5]

A second point about the Eucharist's doctrine of eucharistic presence is to remember that in the reception of the Eucharist we are not receiving a divine thing or object, we are encountering a person, the risen Christ. The question to ask regarding the Eucharist is not, "What are we receiving?" but "Who are we encountering?" Catholics have long since turned the word *communion* into an object as in the phrase, "receiving holy Communion," when it originally referred to a relationship, as in the statement, "We are being drawn into communion with Christ."

As servants of the eucharistic mystery, lay eucharistic ministers can do much in the manner of exercising their ministry to assist the community in coming to an affirmation of Christ's sacramental presence. First, lay eucharistic ministers must recall that they are not keepers/dispensers of a sacred object but servants of a mystery. While reverence for the eucharistic species is indispensable, it must not turn into a scrupulous obsession, for example, with avoiding dropping a crumb of the consecrated bread or spilling a drop of the consecrated wine. To offer Communion is just that, it is to assist the assembly in their entrance into communion with the risen Lord by means of the sacred meal. The focus is on the communion with Christ made possible by this meal we share, it is not on the eucharistic elements themselves. The celebration of the Eucharist involves a personal encounter with Christ, and eucharistic ministers can help facilitate this encounter by the dignity with which they offer the eucharistic elements but even more with the way in which they make eye contact with communicants— the person of the minister and the person of the communicant meeting in the acknowledgment of their shared personal communion with the person of Christ. The lay eucharistic minister fosters nothing less than communion with God in Christ by the power of the Holy Spirit.

QUESTIONS FOR REFLECTION

How have you been raised to understand the doctrine of real presence?

Does this reflection challenge that viewpoint in any way?

Do you see your ministry as one in which you are called to invite people into communion with Christ?

The Eucharist as Sacrifice

A second eucharistic conviction of Roman Catholicism holds that we do not just receive Christ in the Eucharist, we receive the one who has offered himself to us and for us as gift. Traditionally we have affirmed this under the category of sacrifice. This doctrine reminds us that Jesus offered himself as bread for the world in his complete fidelity to his Father, accepting that fidelity to the will of the Father, in the face of human sin, might lead to death, death on a cross. At every celebration of the Eucharist we believe that we are sacramentally sharing in that once-and-for all gift of Christ on the cross. Christ's self-gift on the cross has become an eternal reality, and every celebration of the Eucharist shares in the reality of that gift, not just as something that happened two thousand years ago but as a present reality.

Past understandings of the eucharistic sacrifice were often subject to a kind of mechanistic view of the sacrament. The idea seemed to be that with each celebration of the Mass a new "quantity" of grace was "injected" into the world. This led to a disastrous view that Masses must be said as frequently as possible to maximize the grace thereby produced. The ancient tradition of offering a Mass for an individual as a profound corporate response to the biblical injunction that we pray for one another soon gave way to a view of the Eucharist as a kind of ecclesial "grace-dispenser." This notion, however piously embraced, is far removed from the true significance of the sacrificial dimension of the Eucharist. To say the Eucharist is a sacrifice is not to suggest that we are somehow re-sacrificing Christ, but that, by way of the sacrament, the one sacrifice of Christ on the cross is being made real and effective here and now.

The sacrificial dimension of the Eucharist reminds us that the Eucharist is above all an *action* in which we encounter Christ, not in a passive or static fashion but as the one who gives himself to us here and now. In the Eucharist, we are drawn into Christ's paschal mystery, our name for Christ's movement from life to death to life in the cross and resurrection. In this mystery we discover the great truth that the way of life comes, paradoxically, only through death. What we celebrate in word and sacrament at Mass is nothing other than the deep grammar of the Christian life. For what transpired in the last days of Jesus' life on earth was but a dramatic manifestation of a pattern of life, an interior movement, that characterized all of Jesus' life. He always acted in perfect accord with an interior spiritual rhythm that we might characterize simply as life—death—life. The central challenge of Christian life is to internalize and make this spiritual rhythm our own. With Jesus we are to *live* out of the assurance that we are God's good creatures, *die* to any tendency to make ourselves the ultimate reality in the universe, and *live* anew in lives of loving attentiveness and service to others. What Jesus lived, he also taught. "Unless a grain of wheat falls into the earth and dies, it remains just a single grain; but if it dies, it bears much fruit" (John 12:24). In his life and in his teaching, he offered us a new vision of human wholeness in which "death" and "life" are infused with new meaning. We are thus introduced to the peculiar program for Christian living. If you want to be happy, seek the happiness of others. If you would be fulfilled, abandon the quest for fulfillment.

To delight in the gifts of creation, you must learn on occasion to abstain from them. To know the joy of the feast, you must embrace the longing that arises from the fast. This is the mystery that we celebrate at each Eucharist.

At least since the Middle Ages, changes in eucharistic practice have led to the lamentable situation in which Catholics view the Eucharist as an object (for example, the host which is to be reserved) or as a devotion (adoration of the Blessed Sacrament whether within the Mass or outside of it) rather than as an action of Christ acting in and through the Eucharist. As we discussed above, we Catholics have a strong and enduring commitment to what we call the doctrine of Real Presence. But this belief flows out of *prior* convictions regarding what Christ is *doing* in the Eucharist.

A failure to grasp this is often evident in one of the great sources of controversy that emerges whenever a new church is being built or an old one renovated, namely the question of where the tabernacle ought to be located. Whatever decision a local community comes to, it must be grounded in a solid eucharistic theology. This theology must begin with the following sacramental principle, namely, that *it is the action of the eucharistic celebration that provides the framework for understanding eucharistic devotion and not vice versa.* Our rich tradition of eucharistic adoration can only be understood within the framework of the eucharistic liturgy proper. I once heard a priest justify the placement of the tabernacle immediately behind and above the altar with the explanation that the tabernacle should be given greater prominence than the altar because, "after all, Christ is only present on the altar for a few moments; He is present in the tabernacle perpetually." This perspective forgets that we do not just believe in Christ's eucharistic presence, we believe that Christ's eucharistic presence is salvific. That is, Christ does not merely passively abide in the host and precious blood under the appearance of bread and wine. Rather Christ is disclosed for us as the one "broken and poured out." It is in the eucharistic action, not in the tabernacle, that we come to discover that Christ is actively giving himself to us in this sacramental participation in the paschal mystery. It is the paschal mystery that offers us the distinctive logic of the Eucharist. Christ is never just "present on the altar." Christ is on the altar as gift being offered for us and spiritual food nourishing us. When the tabernacle and eucharistic adoration is allowed to displace both the altar and the eucharistic celebration in the liturgical life of the parish, the sacramental imagination of the parish is likely to suffer and an inevitable tendency to reduce the Eucharist to a mere object to be adored will follow. When, however, a carefully prepared eucharistic celebration is the center of the parish's liturgical life, eucharistic adoration will flow from it as grateful Catholics gather to adore the one who offers himself as gift for us. Here adoration will lead one to recollect the table from which this food came and the mission given to those who feasted at that table to go into the world and love as Christ loved.

This failure to understand the primacy of the eucharistic action in the Mass is being exacerbated by the increase in parishes that must rely on only Communion services because they have no resident priest. It is even blurred by the all-too-frequent practice of distributing Communion from the Eucharist reserved in the tabernacle rather than consecrating a sufficient number of hosts so that all the faithful gathered may, as the liturgical documents remind us, receive from the transformed gifts they have offered at that liturgy.

It should go without saying that at the core of the spirituality of any eucharistic minister must be a deep appreciation for this paschal mystery. When someone approaches a eucharistic minister for Communion, what they will be given is nothing less than Christ offering himself as bread for the world and Christ inviting the communicant and the entire community to enter into the realm of gift and self-gift as the way of the reign of God.

QUESTION FOR REFLECTION

If we are encountering Christ in the Eucharist as God's self-gift to the world, what do you think ought to be our own response to this gift when, at the end of each Mass, we are ourselves sent out into the world?

"Receive What You Are"

✠ ✠ ✠

The Eucharist is no private encounter, it is the event and action of the whole community. The early Christian community was alive to the insight that in the celebration of the Eucharist Christ was made present not only in the eucharistic elements but in the eucharistic community. As the church receives Christ's body in the Eucharist so too it becomes the body of Christ in and for the world. Saint Augustine puts the matter most eloquently in one of his many sermons:

> *Since you are the Body of Christ and His members, it is your mystery that is placed on the Lord's table, it is your mystery that you receive. You reply "Amen" to that which you are, and by replying you consent.... Be what you see, and receive what you are.* [6]

We become Christ as we receive Christ in the Eucharist. To affirm this profound insight is immediately to avoid the dangers of both horizontalism (exclusive focus on community formation) and verticalism (exclusive focus on one's individual relationship with God) that were mentioned earlier. We avoid liturgical horizontalism when we realize that at the Eucharist we are not a self-made community; we are not individuals who gather together to make a church. Rather, through the celebration of the Eucharist, Christ makes us his very body, his sacramental presence before the world. This insight also avoids liturgical verticalism because it reminds us that the Eucharist is no private encounter with Christ, it is a communal event in which we *as a community* become Christ.

Eucharistic ministers are mindful of this great truth when, in offering the Eucharist to communicants, they follow the rubrics and acclaim, "The body of Christ," and not, as many do, "This is the body of Christ." The former proclamation affirms that not only is Christ present in the eucharistic elements but that, in consuming the Eucharist, we are all corporately becoming Christ. To be a lay eucharistic minister is to participate in the very building up of the church as the body of Christ.

QUESTIONS FOR REFLECTION

How does your community affirm this important insight that "we become what we receive"?

Can you think of anything concretely that eucharistic ministers could do differently in order to better affirm this important insight?

The Eucharist and
the Reign of God
✠ ✠ ✠

An appreciation of the ecclesial dimension of the Eucharist leads us to a broader appreciation for the relationship between the Eucharist and the reign of God. The church's celebration of the Eucharist is grounded not only in the Last Supper but also in Jesus' practice of table fellowship with sinners. In first century Judaism, the table fellowship was a ritual meal that celebrated God's communion with God's people. By celebrating such a meal with outcasts and sinners, Jesus overturned the conventional religious understanding of table fellowship that stressed a communion among the ritually pure. This rejection of first-century ritual exclusivism leads us to the ethical dimension of every celebration of the Eucharist. If Jesus' table fellowship overthrew social conventions that distinguished between insiders and outsiders, does not the Eucharist place similar ethical demands on us? This sense of the ethical dimensions placed on us by the Eucharist is certainly in Saint Paul's understanding. His First Letter to the Corinthians reveals his strong conviction that, for communities shaped by the celebration of the Eucharist, certain communal practices were no longer appropriate. For example, he condemns an attitude of carousing and gluttony in which some overate while others went hungry (see 1 Corinthians 11:17-22). Indeed Paul's admonishments suggest that some social stratification within the Corinthian community may have endured wherein the poor did not have equal access to Eucharist. Eugene LaVerdiere speculates that the wealthy may have eaten in a separate room from the poor prior to the celebration of the Eucharist. If so, then Paul's warning that the Corinthians' celebration of the Eucharist may be bringing about their condemnation may have been a stern warning that this social stratification of rich and poor was not in keeping with the behaviors appropriate to those who had entered into the covenant of Christ. They are eating the bread and drinking the cup "unworthily." Note that for Paul the question is not one of irreverence in the reception of the Eucharist itself (a common concern today); the Corinthian community was irreverent because of their divisions and unjust practices.[7]

The Eucharist's foundation in Jesus' preaching of the reign of God suggests that we need to stress much more the demands for justice within our communities and in our world that the celebration of the Eucharist places on us. As the late Father Robert Hovda was so fond of pointing out, at the celebration of each liturgy the Christian community is "playing the reign of God." It is that time, once a week, in which we act "as if" God's reign had really come.

Good liturgical celebration, like a parable, takes us by the hair of our heads, lifts us momentarily out of the cesspool of injustice we call home, puts us in the promised and challenging reign of God, where we are treated like we have never been treated anywhere else...where we are bowed to and sprinkled and censed and kissed and touched and where we share equally among all a holy food and drink.[8]

We are then sent forth in mission in service of God's reign. I know one parish that tried to emphasize this connection by inviting parishioners, immediately after the liturgy, to proceed to the parish center and participate in making lunches for the homeless. The connection between our nourishment at the table of the Lord and our need to offer nourishment to others was made all the more real by this communal action. Any spirituality of the eucharistic minister will be defective that does not also attend to the Eucharist's commitment to justice and care for the least as a demand placed on us by our celebration of the Eucharist itself.

QUESTION FOR REFLECTION

How does your community make connections between the celebration of the Eucharist and the call to serve the coming reign of God in the work for peace and justice?

Extending Table Fellowship: Communion with the Sick

✠ ✠ ✠

We considered earlier the adoration of the Blessed Sacrament. This practice has its origins in the early church practice of reserving the Blessed Sacrament in a sacred place for the interim between the celebration of the eucharistic liturgy itself and the time in which a minister of the church could bring the Eucharist to those who because of illness or other infirmity were unable to attend. Today lay eucharistic ministers often engage in the practice of bringing Communion to the sick. This important ministry is one of extending table fellowship. The table fellowship of the local community is, as it were, widened to include those who may not be physically present because of illness and infirmity. This means that when a eucharistic minister brings Communion to them they are extending the eucharistic ministry. What was begun at the altar of the local church is extended to hospital rooms and nursing homes. Consequently, the eucharistic minister is bringing to the sick and infirm not just the eucharistic elements but the fellowship of the eucharistic community. The visitation should be a tangible expression of that fellowship. The Scripture readings for that Sunday feast should be read, the sick and infirm should be invited to unite their prayers to the prayers of the faithful who gathered physically around the eucharistic banquet table that Sunday. The news and concerns of the community should be shared with the communicants. In short, every attempt should be made by the eucharistic minister to communicate that what is being brought is nothing less than the local community's table fellowship. What is being shared is eucharistic Communion with Christ in union with the whole people of God. This means that in a very profound way eucharistic ministers, in bringing Communion to the sick and infirm are in fact bearers of the spirit of the church itself, they are ministers of eucharistic hospitality. The true character of this vital ministry is effectively ritualized in those parishes where eucharistic ministers to the sick and infirm are called to the altar during the Sunday Eucharist to receive the hosts and are sent out by the presider in the presence of the entire gathered assembly.

Conclusion

✠ ✠ ✠

C atholics rightly believe that the Eucharist is "the summit toward which the activity of the church is directed; it is also the source from which all its power flows."[9] The role of the lay eucharistic minister, as with all liturgical ministers, is to serve the community in its liturgical celebration. It is easy for all of us to domesticate the liturgy, to tame it or rob it of its transformative power. This can happen when we come to the celebration ill prepared or when those responsible for its celebration fail to fulfill their responsibility to be servants of the mystery and servants of the community. I am reminded of Annie Dillard, that great American author and naturalist, who remarked wryly on her experience of attending many Catholic liturgies.

Why do we people in churches seem like cheerful, brainless tourists on a packaged tour of the Absolute?...On the whole, I do not find Christians, outside of the catacombs, sufficiently sensible of conditions. Does anyone have the foggiest idea what sort of power we so blithely invoke? Or, as I suspect, does no one believe a word of it? The churches are children playing on the floor with their chemistry sets, mixing up a batch of TNT to kill a Sunday morning. It is madness to wear ladies' straw hats and velvet hats to church; we should all be wearing crash helmets. Ushers should issue life preservers and signal flares; they should lash us to our pews. For the sleeping god may wake someday and take offense, or the waking god may draw us out to where we can never return.[10]

All liturgical ministers must recover a belief in the "power we so blithely invoke." What we do each Sunday when we gather together is indeed intended to draw us "out to where we can never return;" it is intended to change us as we submit ourselves to God's graceful action in our lives and strive to become Christ's servants in the world. It is a dangerous thing to believe, to really believe, that "we become what we receive." As eucharistic ministers, we must have the courage to be servants in the risky business of our transformation into God's people.

QUESTION FOR REFLECTION

What are some ways in which we can tame or domesticate the liturgy, and thereby rob it of its power?

ENDNOTES

1. Nathan Mitchell, *Real Presence: The Work of Eucharist* (Chicago: Liturgy Training Publications, 1998), 28. Mitchell offers a most helpful analysis of the catechism's treatment of the Eucharist, 5-40.

3. ST IIIa, a.75, q.1 *ad primum* as quoted in Mitchell, 112.

4. This reading of the Emmaus story is indebted to Louis-Marie Chauvet, *The Sacraments* (Collegeville: The Liturgical Press, 2001), 23-5.

5. Ibid., 25.

6. Saint Augustine, *Sermon 272* (PL 38:1246-1248).

7. Eugene LaVerdiere, *The Eucharist in the New Testament and the Early Church* (Collegeville: The Liturgical Press, 1996).

8. Robert Hovda, *The Amen Corner* (Collegeville: The Liturgical Press, 1994), 220.

9. The Second Vatican Council's Constitution on the Sacred Liturgy, *Sacrosanctum concilium,* # 10.

10. Annie Dillard, *Teaching a Stone to Talk* (New York: HarperCollins, 1982), 58-9.